Renewable Reality

Guiding Your Venture into Renewable Energy Business

Table of Contents

Chapter 1. Introduction

Navigating the renewable energy landscape can seem daunting, like setting sail on an unfamiliar sea. Fear not, our Special Report titled "Renewable Reality: Guiding Your Venture into Renewable Energy Business," has been crafted with both the novice and the experienced entrepreneur in mind. This comprehensive report aims to demystify the intricacies of investing and operating in the renewable energy sector, making the technical jargon palatable and digestible for anyone willing to take the plunge. Drawing from reliable sources and experts in the field, we endeavor to provide valuable insights into the potential, risks, and dynamism of the renewable energy industry. Both enlightening and practical, this report will inspire you to set sail with confidence into the emerald seas of renewable energy business. Your exciting new venture awaits you!

Chapter 2. An Overview of Renewable Energy: History and Current Landscape

The story of man harnessing renewable energy predates the usage of fossil fuels and reaches back into early civilization, playing a crucial yet under-recognized role in the emergence of modern society. The past century, however, has seen an unprecedented escalation in the pace and scale of renewable energy development, forever altering our energy landscape.

2.1. The First Harnessers of Renewable Energy

From as early as 200 B.C., humanity has been manipulating renewable energy in various ingenious ways. The Greeks, mighty sailors they were, learned to use wind power to navigate their ships across the Aegean Sea. Later on, ingenious inventors found ways to harness the power of water to grind grain - echoing the earliest utility of renewable energy.

In more recent developments, in the 7th century, massive windmills were built in Persia while the concept of harnessing solar energy began to gain recognition with Swiss polymath Johann Heinrich Goethe contriving the 'Goethe house,' a space designed to capture and store the energy radiated by the sun. Biomass, a resource as old as humanity itself, remained crucial throughout history, with organic materials burned to create heat energy.

2.2. The Birth of Modern Renewable Energy: Early 20th Century Developments

Early 20th century scientifically and increasingly, politically, saw the birth of modern renewable energy. In the 1900s, American inventor Charles Fritts constructed the first solar cells, laying the groundwork for contemporary solar photovoltaic technology. However, it was not until the 1930s that hydroelectric power took a significant leap forward with the completion of the Hoover Dam, which remains a beacon of renewable energy capability.

2.3. The Oil Crisis Spur: A Turning Point in Energy History

Fast-forward to the hydrocarbon epoch in the 1960s and 70s; dependency on fossil fuels developed rapidly with oil, coal, and natural gas providing over 90% of global energy needs. These sources, though abundantly profitable, were soon to reveal their volatility with the 1973 oil crisis.

A geopolitical situation that led to a dramatic surge in oil prices caused the world to consider the vulnerability of relying solely on fossil fuels for energy. Consequently, research and development kicked into high gear, leading to exponential improvements in renewable energy technologies such as solar panels and wind turbines.

2.4. From the 80s to the 21st Century: A Wider Acceptance

The 1980s-90s signified a period of wider acceptance and early commercialization of renewable technology, with the development of solar, wind, and geothermal installations. Importantly, renewable energy started featuring more prominently in government policies, regulatory frameworks, and deeper social discourse. The emphasis grew gradually on the urgency of reducing greenhouse gas emissions, thereby influencing a shift towards low-carbon, renewable energy sources.

The entrance into the 21st century saw renewable energy receiving more substantial attention as adverse climate change impacts and the need for energy security propelled rapid growth in the sector. Various governments set ambitious targets for renewable energy, and massive investments in technology and infrastructure followed. Now, renewable energy is considered not just an alternative but a crucial part of the global energy matrix.

2.5. Renewable Energy Today: A Rapidly Changing Landscape

In this present epoch, the renewable energy landscape has transformed dramatically, and its significance is more prominent than ever. With the increasing urgency to combat climate change coupled with the economic feasibility of renewable energy technologies, the world is pivoting towards a more sustainable, renewable energy-centric future.

Wind energy, solar photovoltaic, hydroelectric power, biomass, and geothermal energy have all come leaps and bounds in the last few decades. The price per kilowatt-hour (kWh) for these renewable sources has plummeted, making them directly competitive with fossil fuel energy sources in many areas.

Historically, renewable energy was often considered circular, limited to remote locations or for niche applications due to the sporadic nature of resources like wind and sun. However, the evolution of technology and grid infrastructure has revolutionized the way we generate and distribute electricity, enabling renewables to become a dependable, widespread energy source.

To navigate the future of renewables, it's crucial to recognize the role of digital transformation, artificial intelligence, and advanced storage technologies. These elements combined have the potential to enhance renewable energy management considerably, optimizing energy production, and forecasting demand with precision.

2.6. To the Future: Predictions and Possibilities

Looking forward, renewable energy technologies are poised to play a central role in combating climate change and achieving sustainable energy security. The integration of renewables in various economies is well underway, and it is expected that by 2050, renewables could provide up to 85% of global electricity.

The future will see a far greater reliance on technology and digitalization to optimize renewable energy. The integration of blockchain technology could further revolutionize the sector by enabling transparent, decentralized energy trading, and technologies like quantum computing could further enhance the forecasting accuracy and performance of renewables.

In conclusion, the journey of renewable energy has been as vibrant and dynamic as the energy it harnesses. The technologically advanced, environmentally aware world of today has realized the potential locked away within nature for millennia - the potential of renewable energy. With the landscape evolving continually and rapidly, the central role of renewable energy in our future is no longer a topic of debate but a certainty that we are steadily progressing towards.

Chapter 3. Types of Renewable Energy: Harnessing Nature's Bounty

Renewable energy, as its name suggests, is energy that has been derived from Earth's natural resources, replenishing at a faster rate than they are being consumed. The sun, wind, water, geothermal heat, and certain types of biomass are among the most commonly used sources of renewable energy. Each source comes with a unique set of benefits and considerations. The following sections provide an in-depth analysis of the major types of renewable energy and how we harness them.

3.1. Solar Energy

Solar energy, harnessed via the sun, is by far the most abundant source of renewable energy available. It has the potential to provide more than enough energy to meet global needs if properly harnessed. Solar energy is captured primarily through solar photovoltaic (PV) panels. These panels consist of solar cells that convert sunlight directly into electricity.

The implementation of solar energy varies greatly, from small rooftop systems operated by individuals to large solar farms that feed power into the electrical grid. The viability of solar power is influenced by the availability of sunlight, which can be affected by geographic location, season, time of day, and local weather patterns.

The cost of solar PVs has fallen dramatically over the past few years, making solar power a financially viable option in many parts of the world. In addition to producing electricity, solar energy can be used for heating purposes. Solar thermal systems can be used to heat water for personal use, space heating, or even generation of steam to drive turbines.

3.2. Wind Energy

Wind energy, as the name suggests, is extracted by harnessing the power of the wind. It can often be seen in the form of wind turbines dotting rural landscapes. Wind turbines work on a simple principle: the wind turns the turbine's propeller-like blades, which spins a shaft connected to a generator that produces electricity.

The efficiency of a wind turbine largely depends on the speed and consistency of the wind. Therefore, the topography and climatic conditions of the area significantly impact the productivity of wind energy systems. Similar to solar energy, wind energy can be harvested on a small scale, such as a single home or business, or on a large scale like wind farms that sell the electricity on the power grid.

The advancement in technology and drop in prices has made wind energy competitive with traditional forms of power generation. Moreover, wind turbines can be installed on land or offshore, adding to its versatility while improving aesthetics and minimizing noise complaints.

3.3. Hydroelectric Energy

Hydroelectric power is the most widely used form of renewable energy around the world, contributing to about half of the global renewable electricity. There are two primary methods used to generate hydroelectric power: conventional hydroelectric and run-of-the-river systems. Both systems involve diverting the flow of water to spin a turbine connected to a power generator.

The size of these systems can vary from massive projects like the Hoover Dam to micro-hydro installations suitable for a small community or even as a standalone system for an individual home.

However, the construction of large dams used for conventional hydroelectric power can have significant environmental impacts, such as changes to existing habitats, and may lead to the displacement of people living in the area.

3.4. Geothermal Energy

Geothermal energy is derived from the heat below Earth's surface. This heat can be sourced from shallow ground to hot water and hot rock found a few miles underneath the Earth's surface, and even farther down to the extremely high temperatures of molten rock called magma.

In a geothermal power plant, a well is drilled into a geothermal reservoir to provide a steady and sustained supply of steam and hot water, which is used to drive a turbine linked to an electricity generator. The spent steam and hot water can be pumped back into the reservoir to maintain pressure and extend the life of the geothermal source.

Geothermal power plants, unlike solar and wind systems, provide a constant source of power, as the energy does not vary with changes in weather or daily cycles. However, location is a significant factor in the viability of geothermal energy, since it requires hot ground temperatures that are not found worldwide.

3.5. Biomass Energy

Biomass energy, also commonly known as bioenergy, is derived from organic materials, particularly plant or animal matter. Examples of biomass fuels include wood, crops, manure, and some types of garbage.

When these materials are burned, chemical energy is released as heat and can be used to create power. Biomass can also be converted into other usable forms of energy like methane gas or transportation fuels like ethanol and biodiesel.

While the process of burning biomass releases carbon dioxide, a greenhouse gas, the growth of plants used in biomass energy production absorbs a roughly equivalent amount of CO_2, meaning the impact on global warming can be considered neutral. However, ethical and sustainable sourcing of biomass is a crucial factor to consider to ensure the net carbon emissions remain low.

In conclusion, each variety of renewable energy has its own benefits, challenges, and requirements. Understanding these different types can guide businesses and individuals towards making informed decisions when it comes to investing in or using renewable resources. The continued evolution and technological advancement in renewable energy sources will provide even more options for harnessing nature's bounty in ways that are both profitable and sustainable.

Chapter 4. The Economics of Renewable Energy: Understanding Return on Investment

To grasp the dynamics of the renewable energy sector's economic aspects, primarily focusing on understanding Return on Investment (ROI), this segment delves into diverse financial and economic determinants. These include the cost of different energy generation methods, government policies and incentives, cost-benefit analysis, and potential risks.

4.1. Cost Analysis: Traditional vs Renewable energy

With the advancement of technology, the costs associated with energy production from renewable sources are steadily decreasing, making them a competitively viable alternative to traditional energy sources. Several factors influence the cost dynamics of different energy generation methods. These include initial startup costs, fuel prices, maintenance needs, capacities, efficiencies, and lifespans.

While conventional energy sources frequently bear lower upfront costs, their operational expenses can be unpredictable due to fluctuations in fuel prices and high maintenance needs. On the other hand, renewable energy technologies typically involve higher setup costs, largely due to the specialized equipment required. However, they possess lower running expenses due to free or low-cost fuel sources (such as the sun, wind, or water) and minimal maintenance needs.

Though the present focus on climate change has raised the number of renewable energy projects, a considerable part of the equation in an investor's decision-making process remains profitability.

4.2. Understanding Return on Investment in Renewable Energy

ROI in renewable energy is derived from various components, including capital cost, operating expenses, total energy output over a project's lifespan, and project revenue. It's essential to account for all these elements when calculating ROI to get an accurate estimate.

To calculate the ROI, the total revenue from the project is divided by the total initial investment. The resulting number, typically expressed as a percentage, forms the ROI. A higher ROI indicates a more profitable investment.

However, estimating an accurate ROI may be challenging due to the unpredictability of some variables, such as energy prices, subsidies, and other incentive schemes. Therefore, it's advisable to conduct a sensitivity analysis to consider various scenarios that might unfold during the project's lifespan.

4.3. Government Policies and Incentives

Government policies and incentives can have a significant impact on the ROI for renewable energy projects. These might include Feed-in Tariffs (FiTs), Power Purchase Agreements (PPAs), tax credits, or other incentive schemes designed to encourage investment in renewable energy.

FiTs guarantee a certain payment to renewable energy producers for each unit of energy produced. Similarly, PPAs provide a framework where energy producers commit to supply a certain amount of power at a fixed price for a long-term period. Tax credits provide a direct reduction on taxes paid by the renewable energy producer, which can fundamentally enhance ROI.

While these incentives can improve the profitability of renewable energy projects significantly, it's essential to consider their sustainability in the long run. Potential changes in policy could negatively impact the ROI.

4.4. Risk Assessment and Mitigation

Like any investment, renewable energy projects carry risks that can affect the ROI. Some common risks include technology failure, lower than anticipated energy output due to weather patterns, delays in project completion, changes in government policy, and uncertainties in energy prices.

Identifying these risks, assessing their potential impact, and implementing effective mitigation strategies is crucial in optimizing ROI. Employing a robust risk management strategy can maximize returns and minimize potential losses.

Further, understanding how risks can change over time is crucial. During the development phase, risks associated with permits, financing, and contracting are paramount. However, during operation, project performance, operating and maintenance costs become more prominent.

4.5. Cost-Benefit Analysis

Taking everything into account, a thorough cost-benefit analysis is critical in understanding the potential ROI. This process should include evaluation of upfront costs, estimated revenues, operational costs, government incentives, potential risks and mitigation strategies, and sensitivity analysis.

Though ROI can serve as an effective measure of an investment's attractiveness, other factors such as contributions to green credentials, energy security, and social engagement should not be overlooked. After all, sustainable investments resonate with broader environmental, social, and governance objectives that extend beyond mere financial considerations.

Navigating the renewable energy landscape appears complex. However, comprehensive analysis and understanding of key economic and financial aspects can significantly aid in making informed decisions that could yield high returns, both monetarily and in terms of positive impact on the environment. While the initial plunge may seem intimidating, with due diligence and astute strategizing, it is possible to achieve a prosperous and sustainable voyage in the realm of renewable energy business.

Chapter 5. Technological Advances: Keeping Pace with Innovation

In the unrelenting current of technological developments, keeping pace with innovation in the renewable energy sector is an absolute essentiality. Whether we delve into the multifaceted prospects of solar energy or explore the imposing power of the wind, advancements in technology are at the core of our journey towards harnessing renewable power.

5.1. Mastering Solar Technologies

Solar energy represents one of the most abundant and underutilized sources of renewable energy on the planet. With technological trends shifting towards efficiency and scalability, photovoltaics (PV) and concentrating solar power (CSP) have taken significant strides.

In photovoltaics, we have witnessed a shift from traditional mono and polycrystalline silicon models to thin-film solar cells and newer advancements, such as multi-junction and perovskite solar cells. These advancements aim to increase the efficiency of solar cells, with potential efficiencies of over 40% in lab conditions for multi-junction cells. A part of this innovation drive also emphasizes cost effectiveness, reducing the dependence on expensive materials, like silver, in solar cell manufacturing.

Concentrating solar power (CSP), on the other hand, focuses on large scale power generation. CSP plants use mirrors to concentrate sunlight onto receivers that collect solar energy and convert it to heat. The heat energy can then be used to produce electricity through a steam turbine or heat engine. Molten salt technology is being leveraged in CSP for energy storage, enabling power generation even in the absence of sunlight.

5.2. Shaping the Winds of Change

Technology in wind energy, like solar, has seen staggering advancements. Onshore wind technology remains a focus area, with increasing turbine size and enhanced designs leading to greater efficiency and power output. The average rotor diameter and hub height have increased in the past decade, thereby boosting the capacity of modern wind turbines.

Offshore wind energy, although more complex, bodes well for markets with coastal access, thanks to its higher yield and reduced impact on residential landscapes. The rise of floating wind turbines substitutes the need for fixed foundations, thus allowing their deployment in deeper waters and opening up new potential sites for wind farms.

5.3. Harnessing the Tides

Energy from tides and waves is emerging as a promising renewable resource. Tidal stream technologies, for example, act akin to underwater wind turbines, while wave energy converters utilize the kinetic energy of water's movement. Additionally, the predictability of tides grants this energy source a consistency not found in solar or wind energy.

Micro-hydro systems, although not new, are seeing a resurgence interest. As an off-grid solution, it appeals to regions without mainstream power infrastructure. These systems, by capitalizing on small water flows rather than large dams, are sustainable, low-impact, and can function year-round.

5.4. Embracing our Geothermal Future

Geothermal energy, the heat from the Earth's core, is a massive untapped energy resource. Enhanced Geothermal Systems (EGS) are gaining attention for their potential to provide a significant portion of our energy needs. EGS, in contrast to traditional geothermal wells, create reservoirs of permeable rock to allow the extraction of heat from deeper, hotter regions.

Innovations in drilling technology also promise a bright future for geothermal. Deep drilling technology might result in more cost-effective extraction methods, while the prospect of using supercritical geothermal systems is exciting.

5.5. Storing Energy: The Paradigm Shift

While advancements in energy generation technology are vital, the future lies in efficient energy storage solutions. Newer, more robust, and efficient battery technologies, from lithium-ion batteries to promising research in solid-state batteries, offer improved performance.

Energy storage also extends beyond batteries. Pumped hydro storage, for example, uses gravity as a means of storing energy, while thermal storage collects and stores heat for later use.

Technological advancements and subsequent shifts in market dynamics have made renewable energy more accessible and prevalent. The future of renewable technology is set on a positive trajectory, with plentiful opportunities and considerable growth potential. Navigating this landscape can seem daunting, but armed with the right knowledge and a perspective on cutting-edge innovation, your venture can steer confidently into the renewable tomorrow.

Chapter 6. Policy Impact: Navigating Legal and Regulatory Frameworks

While sailing the vast sea of renewable energy business, one of the most pivotal aspects that entrepreneurs must understand is the legal and regulatory frameworks that shape this landscape. The tide of policies can often turn swiftly, rendering regions either favorable or challenging for renewable energy businesses. Investing time to understand these contexts can act as a compass, securing your venture from unexpected setbacks and navigating you towards safer waters.

6.1. Understanding the Legal Landscape

Knowledge of the legal landscape surrounding renewable energy is an essential prerequisite for any budding venture. A thorough grasp of the variety and nuances of legal instruments, such as renewable portfolio standards, feed-in tariffs, tax credits, and public benefit funds, among others, can lay a strong foundation for your journey.

Renewable Portfolio Standards (RPS) mandate that utility companies produce a certain percentage of their electricity from renewable sources, encouraging a shift towards clean energy production. On the other hand, Feed-in Tariffs (FiTs) guarantee set payments to renewable energy producers for the power they generate and feed into the grid, fostering micro-level inventiveness in the sector.

Navigating the landscape of tax credits such as the Investment Tax Credit (ITC) and the Production Tax Credit (PTC) can offer financial rewards for renewable ventures. While ITC provides a tax credit based on capital investment in renewable energy, PTC offers a per-kilowatt-hour (kWh) credit for electricity generated by renewable sources.

Public Benefit Funds (PBFs), set up in certain states, fuel renewables by channeling system benefits charges on electric utilities towards renewable energy projects. By tapping into these funds, ventures can secure much-needed capital to kickstart or expand their operations.

6.2. Regulatory Context: A Double-Edged Sword

Understanding regulations is crucial not just to comply with laws but, more importantly, to identify incentives and constraints offered by various jurisdictions. Regulations can act as both accelerators and barriers for your renewable energy venture, depending on their design and enforcement.

One needs to keep tabs on the fast-evolving regulatory landscape, including permits, regulatory approvals, standards and certifications, and zoning regulations. For instance, permitting requirements may vary between jurisdictions and can be relatively complex, necessitating an extensive application process and adherence to strict building codes and standards.

Regulatory approvals are another area to monitor closely. These approvals, often issued from environmental, energy, infrastructure, or land agencies, legitimise your operations. As the process can sometimes be time-consuming and unpredictable, understanding the nuances can help in accurate planning.

Standards and certifications, like ISO standards or the Leadership in Energy and Environmental Design (LEED) certification, carry significant weight. They not only attest to the quality and sustainability of your business practices and products but may also be necessary for certain markets, thereby driving competitiveness.

Zoning regulations can impact the physical realization of your renewable energy projects, dictating where facilities can be constructed, how much noise they can make, or how tall wind projects can be, among others. A careful study of these regulations can save businesses from future legal repercussions.

6.3. International Climate Agreements: A Guiding Light

Beyond the local context, international climate agreements also shape the renewable energy industry. Key agreements like the Paris Agreement or Kyoto Protocol serve as a compass for nations around the world to transition towards clean energy economies, often setting the tone for domestic policies.

The Paris Agreement, for example, sets ambitious targets for nations to reduce greenhouse gas emissions, driving up demand for renewable energy sources. Nations committed to this pact regularly revisit their strategies, pushing advancements in renewable energy policy.

On the other hand, mechanisms under the Kyoto Protocol, like the Clean Development Mechanism (CDM), offer market-based solutions that can both reduce global emissions and provide financial benefits to renewable energy businesses.

6.4. Policy Innovations: Unchartered Waters

One must also stay abreast of policy innovations that may disrupt the status quo within the renewable energy space. Innovations such as reverse auctions, green banks, or blockchain in energy could harbor transformative potential.

Reverse auctions, where producers bid for long-term contracts to sell power, drive competitive pricing and efficiency within the market. Green banks aim to finance renewable energy projects that traditional banks might deem too risky. Blockchain technology, while still nascent in the sector, could revolutionize the way energy is traded and transactions are documented.

By understanding these facilitating policies and breaking innovations, businesses can chart a more assured path through the renewable energy landscape.

6.5. Tools for Navigating the Policy Impact

Various tools and resources can help in navigating the policy impact in renewable energy business. Useful resources include websites of regulatory agencies, legal databases, policy briefings, industry reports, and academic repositories. Online forums and communities can also provide peer-to-peer insights and collaborative problem-solving.

Managing a renewable energy venture involves sailing through Changing winds, tides, and currents, but with a solid understanding of the legal and regulatory frameworks, the voyage can be rewarding. The more knowledge you acquire in these policy areas, the more you'll be prepared to seize opportunities, mitigate risks, and ultimately succeed in your renewable energy venture. Every journey on this sea begins with thorough preparation. So set your sail and step into the realm of renewable energy, with the compass of policy understanding guiding your way.

Chapter 7. Risk Assessment: Identifying and Mitigating Challenges

Investing in the renewable energy sector can reap immense rewards. As more countries strive for carbon neutrality, renewable energy sources such as wind, solar, hydro, and biomass are becoming increasingly significant. Yet, like all business ventures, there are risks along with the potential for great reward. Thus, a robust risk assessment is vital to identify, understand, and mitigate both financial and operational challenges that may arise throughout the lifecycle of your renewable energy project.

7.1. The Risk Landscape in Renewable Energy Business

There are multiple layers of risk when venturing into renewable energy business, which generally could be categorized into market, credit, operational, and environmental risks.

Market risks are tied to macroeconomic factors that could affect the renewable energy sector, such as changes in government regulations or policies, or fluctuations in energy prices.

Credit risks involve the possibility of nonpayment or delayed payment by buyers or contractual counter-parties.

Operational risks are associated with functional aspects, such as system failures, accidents, or natural disasters that could hamper a project's operation.

Environmental risks encompass potential harm to the environment resulting from the project, which could present regulatory, reputational, or financial problems.

7.2. Identifying Risks: Comprehensive Analysis and Evaluation

Identifying potential risks is the first, crucial step in risk management. Begin by creating a comprehensive inventory of possible threats across every aspect of your project. You might consider utilizing a systematic approach, such as a Risk Breakdown Structure (RBS) or a Failure Modes and Effects Analysis (FMEA).

An RBS categorizes and organizes risks into a hierarchical tree structure, breaking down main risk categories into sub-risks and tying them to specific project elements. For instance, under the market risk category, you could specify sub-risks such as regulatory change risk or energy price volatility risk.

An FMEA, on the other hand, determines how ways your project could fail, the potential effects of each failure, and then assigns each failure mode a risk priority number based on its severity, occurrence, and detectability.

7.3. Evaluating Risks: Understanding Potential Impact and Probability

Once you have identified potential risks, it's time to understand their impact and likelihood. One common technique for evaluating risks is the Risk Impact/Probability Chart, which plots risks on a two-dimensional grid, with impact on the vertical axis and likelihood on the horizontal axis. This creates a visual map of risks and can help prioritize response strategies.

7.4. Mitigating Risks: Strategies and Solutions

The nature of your collected and now assessed risks will guide the development of mitigation strategies. Commonly used risk mitigation methods include avoidance, reduction, transfer, and acceptance.

Avoidance entails changing project plans to sidestep a particular risk, while reduction aims to lessen the impact or probability of a risk. Transfer involves shifting the risk to another entity, often using insurance, while acceptance means recognizing and making preparation for the risk if it materializes.

7.5. Managing Market and Credit Risks

The ever-evolving landscape of policies and prices can pose unique challenges to renewable energy businesses. Active policy monitoring and networking with policymakers and industry experts will help manage market risks.

Credit risks can be mitigated by thorough counterparty risk assessment before entering into agreements and contracts. Attempt robust due diligence, considering credit-rating, financial health, past payment performances, and ongoing business competence.

7.6. Managing Operational and Environmental Risks

An integral part of operational risk management is regular system maintenance and safety inspections, along with comprehensive staff training. A well-prepared disaster recovery plan can guard against natural calamities and accidents.

Environmental risks require balanced management, entailing rigorous compliance with environmental laws, robust waste management systems, and periodic auditing of environmental performance.

7.7. Conclusion

A conscientious approach to risk identification, evaluation and mitigation forms the basis of resilient and sustainable operations in the renewable energy sector. While not all risks can be completely eliminated, a proactive risk management strategy can allow your business to prepare for and properly respond to most hazards, thereby maximizing your chances of success in the emerald seas of this promising industry.

Chapter 8. Case Studies: Success Stories and Lessons Learned

Historically, the concept of deriving energy from renewable resources was relegated to the realm of environmentally conscious enthusiasts and experimental labs. Fast forward to today, however, and we find hundreds of enterprises across the globe creating value by harnessing renewable energy. Let's delve into some success stories while also sharing the lessons learned on these excursions through the emerald seas of renewable energy business.

8.1. Powering Through with Photovoltaics: The Journey of SunPower

In the late 1980s, when photovoltaic technology was still taking its baby steps, Richard Swanson, a Stanford University professor, founded SunPower with a dream of making solar energy mainstream. With their focus on high-efficiency solar cells, SunPower quickly carved a niche for themselves. They rode on the Photovoltaics wave and made waves worldwide with their innovative design. Key contracts with NASA and several utility companies further bolstered their reputation.

Lesson: Specialization can lead to differentiation. By honing in on high-efficiency solar cells, SunPower highlighted the value of focusing on a specific aspect of renewable technology to carve out a solid business proposition.

8.2. Harnessing the Winds of Change: Enercon GmbH

Enercon GmbH, a German manufacturer of wind turbines, was established in 1984. A pioneer in their region, Enercon set the pace by focusing on single gearless type wind turbines. This decision proved invaluable, as their machines demonstrated superior performance in terms of noise reduction and maintenance needs. Today, Enercon is a leading wind turbine manufacturer and continues to invest in research and development to stay ahead.

Lesson: Choosing the right technology base is critical. It enabled Enercon to build a long-term and sustainable competitive advantage through innovation.

8.3. From Wastes to Watts: Waste Management Inc.

Waste Management Inc., with its "waste-to-energy" incinerators, has demonstrated a creative path to renewable energy. The company recycles the heat from burning unavoidable non-recycled waste to generate electricity. Not only does this provide a means to manage waste, but it also creates substantial amounts of renewable energy.

Lesson: Diverse and underexplored opportunities for renewable energy sources lurk everywhere. By creatively redefining waste, the company embellished a traditional business model with a valuable renewable energy component.

8.4. The Game-changing Battery: Tesla's Energy Revolution

Tesla's entry into the renewable energy space highlighted the importance of battery storage solutions. Through innovative battery technology, they've made solar power more practical and dependable - allowing higher efficiency and the ability to store solar power for dull days. The success of the Tesla Powerwall disrupted the entire industry and set a trajectory for future storage solutions.

Lesson: A broad view of the renewable energy chain can open pathways for game-changing advancements. In Tesla's case, the revolution was all about effective power storage.

8.5. Orsted – A Fossil Fuel Company's Transformation

Orsted, a centuries-old Danish energy company, forged a remarkable transformation from fossil fuels to 100% green energy – demonstrating that established energy companies can successfully transition towards renewable sources. Orsted's shift has been rewarded with substantial profitability, while reducing carbon emissions substantially for Denmark.

Lesson: Existing organizations shouldn't fear transformation. Renewables offer a viable business direction, even for traditional enterprises entrenched in fossil fuel usage.

8.6. Hydropower for the Highlands: Scottish Power

Scottish Power, embracing hydropower, has served as a beacon to others interested in this form of renewable energy. Despite the logistical and environmental challenges associated with large-scale hydro projects, Scottish Power has effectively managed these hurdles to produce reliable and sustainable power for many communities.

Lesson: Challenges that seem daunting initially can often be surmountable. A meticulously planned strategy and commitment to sustainability can lead to significant returns on investment.

This journey through remarkable case studies demonstrates the hugely diverse ways in which renewable energy can be harnessed profitably. It illuminates the diversity of strategies that exist within this rapidly growing sector and offers tangible lessons for prospective players keen to delve into renewable ventures. The sea is indeed emerald. Let courage propel your sails!

Chapter 9. The Future of Renewable Energy: Predicting Trends and Opportunities

One cannot talk about the future without first acknowledging the past and understanding the present. As we look into the renewable energy sector, it's crucial to understand the journey that has brought us to the cusp of an energy revolution.

9.1. The Journey So Far

Over the past decade, renewable energy has made significant progress. The increasing recognition of the environmental and economic benefits this form of energy brings, coupled with technology advancements, has catalyzed its growth. From solar panels to wind turbines, advancements in technology have made renewable energy sources more efficient, driving down costs and making them viable alternatives to fossil fuels.

Recent data shows that renewables currently constitute around a quarter of the world's power production. Several countries are championing the use of these sources; for example, Germany generated nearly half of its power from renewable sources in 2020. However, despite these impressive strides, much is left to be done to increase the world's renewable energy capacity in order to counter the looming threat of climate change.

9.2. Prediction Engines: Futuristic Trends in Renewable Energy

With the general trend towards decarbonization and sustainability, and following a close analysis of developments in the sector, there are several key trends we can predict for the future of renewable energy.

Cost-effectiveness: The cost of renewable technologies will continue to decrease. Advancements in technology and economies of scale will make this possible. By reducing costs, renewable energy will assume an increasingly leading role in the power mix of many countries.

Battery technology: The evolution and development of battery storage technology will stimulate the growth of renewable energy. Improved battery storage will mitigate the intermittent nature of certain renewables, particularly solar and wind.

Greater electrification: The electrification rate will surge, driven in part by the proliferation of electric vehicles. This will provide an impetus for the further growth of renewable sources of electricity.

Hydrogen Economy: Hydrogen is now viewed as a potential game-changer in the renewable energy sector. 'Green' hydrogen, produced by electrolysis powered by excess wind and solar power, could prove to be the solution to the energy storage problem, and also serve as a green fuel for industries and transport.

Decentralization and digitization: The advent of technology will allow for decentralized power production and smart grids, paving the way for greater individual and community level energy autonomy, thereby changing the traditional power structure dynamics.

9.3. Unraveling the Opportunities

The shift towards a renewable energy is not without its opportunities. Understanding these can help businesses carve out profitable ventures in the green economy.

Sustainability services: As more organizations seek to reduce their environmental impact and align their operations with SDGs, demand for consulting services in sustainability, environmental impact assessments, and implementation of renewable energy systems will grow.

Technological innovations: The expansion of the renewable sector will necessitate the development of new technologies and solutions. There will be a massive need for efficient energy storage solutions, smart grid systems, and software for managing renewable energy assets.

Financing: Renewable energy projects require financing for development, installation, and operation. Financial institutions with green portfolios and specialized clean-energy investment firms will find ample opportunities in this area.

Renewable energy trading: With the increasing capacity of renewable energy produced worldwide, there will be opportunities for businesses that trade energy credits and potential application of blockchain to the sector to increase efficiency and transparency.

9.4. Risks and Challenges

Like every sector, the renewable energy industry is subject to a number of risks. Firstly, while technology is getting better, some forms of renewable energy are intermittent by nature. Battery technology and grid management must improve to handle this intermittency.

Secondly, as the industry grows, it will face increased resource and supply chain pressures. Renewables are not devoid of environmental impact, and the industry will need to address responsible sourcing and recycling of materials.

Thirdly, while costs are coming down, solar and wind projects still require substantial upfront capital. This calls for innovative financing models to make renewable energy projects more accessible.

Lastly, policy uncertainty can pose significant risks, especially in regions where renewable energy is heavily reliant on government incentives.

Despite these challenges, the future of the renewable energy sector is promising. With collective commitment and continued technological advancement, it's not beyond imagination to envision a world powered primarily by renewable energy. As businesses adapt and pivot to this future, those who properly understand and navigate these terrains will truly be the flag bearers of a sustainable future.

Chapter 10. Sustainability Goals: Aligning your Venture with Global Initiatives

Before undertaking a venture in the renewable energy business, it is essential to acquaint yourself with the global sustainability initiatives. Understanding these initiatives will not only guide your strategic planning and decision-making but also align your venture with the global goals, making it a part of the bigger solution to our energy and climate challenges.

10.1. Understanding Global Sustainability Initiatives

Our planet is at an inflection point. Global initiatives intent on combatting climate change and promoting sustainable development are a response to this crisis concerning the human relationship with the environment. Familiarization with these initiatives is fundamental to understand your position in the global tableau.

The United Nations' Sustainable Development Goals (SDGs) are a universal call to action to end poverty, protect the planet, and ensure that all people enjoy peace and prosperity by 2030. Among these goals, SDG 7 aims to "Ensure access to affordable, reliable, sustainable and modern energy for all". Your renewable energy venture can be an agent of change in accomplishing this specific goal.

The Paris Agreement is another significant global initiative. This binding international treaty on climate change aims to limit the global temperature increase to well below 2 degrees Celsius above pre-industrial levels, and to pursue efforts to limit the temperature increase to 1.5 degrees Celsius. Investing in renewable energy is crucial to achieve this target by reducing greenhouse gas emissions.

10.2. Aligning Your Venture with Global Initiatives

Striving to meet these global initiatives can serve several purposes for your renewable energy enterprise. It is not only the ethical choice but also holds immense business potential. Here's how you can get your venture in line with them.

First, encourage clean energy production and consumption. Ensure energy conservation through your operations, products or services. A clear example could be a company that installs solar panels, consequently reducing the reliance on non-renewable resources.

Second, foster innovation. Developed economies have achieved significant results through technological advantage, and renewable energy is no different. Invest in R&D and technological innovations that make renewable energy as, if not more, viable as conventional sources. For instance, a company could focus on developing more efficient wind turbines or improving energy storage technology.

Third, collaborate with stakeholders. This includes working with governments, non-governmental organizations, and communities to promote renewable energy and its benefits. Collaboration aims at understanding the policy landscape, raising awareness about renewable energy, and driving the adoption of your products or services.

10.3. Capitalizing on Green Business Strategies

Embracing green business strategies can help your renewable energy venture to promote sustainability while bolstering its business performance. Such strategies can encompass:

1. Resource efficiency: This involves the optimal use of resources. For example, using recycled materials in product manufacturing or minimizing waste generated during processes.

2. Energy efficiency: Investments in energy efficiency can result in cost savings. An example could be a company that minimizes electricity consumption in their factories by using LED lighting and energy-efficient equipment.

3. Inclusive business practices: This includes providing opportunities to marginalized communities or adopting equal and fair business practices. For instance, a company could offer jobs to local communities in the construction and maintenance of renewable energy installations.

Further, green business strategies can enhance the image of your enterprise, attracting consumers who value sustainability.

10.4. Measuring Your Impact on Global Sustainability Initiatives

Your renewable energy venture's contributions to global sustainability initiatives can be measured using the Triple Bottom Line (TBL) approach. This concept considers three dimensions: economic, social, and environmental impact.

Economic impact refers to your venture's contribution to the economy. This can be in the form of job creation, taxation, and investments.

The social impact is about improving people's living standards. This can be in the form of energy access to off-grid areas or employment opportunities to marginalized communities.

The environmental impact measures your venture's contribution to climate change mitigation. This can be in the reduction of CO2 emissions or pollution prevention.

Tracking progress on these dimensions will help keep your renewable energy venture on the right path.

Starting a renewable energy venture implies taking a step toward a sustainable future. Aligning your business with global sustainability initiatives places your venture at the heart of the solution to our energy and climate challenges. Develop a green business strategy, measure your impact, and let your venture be the change that the world needs.

Chapter 11. Developing Your Business Plan: Practical Steps towards a Successful Venture

Before embarking on your venture into the renewable energy sector, charting out a robust business plan is paramount. Just like a captain wouldn't set sail into uncharted waters without a map, a responsible entrepreneur doesn't venture into a new business without a thorough plan in place. Let's consider some practical steps towards shaping a successful business plan in the context of renewable energy.

11.1. Understanding the Renewable Energy Sector

The first step towards forming a sustainable plan starts with a deep understanding of the renewable energy sector. This understanding will lay the grounds for the feasibility of your project, offering an insight into the market, technology, regulations, and potential risks linked to your business. Thorough research entails:

1. Evaluating the diverse types of renewable energy sources— solar, wind, hydro, bioenergy, and geothermal— and understanding how each functions in various geographical, climatic, and socio-economic contexts.

2. Assessing market trends, pricing mechanisms, and growth potential within different renewable energy segments, such as utility-scale projects, residential and commercial solar, wind energy projects, among others.

3. Understanding local and global renewable energy policies, subsidies, and regulations, including environmental and

construction permits.

11.2. Identifying the Business Objective

Having charted the landscape, you must now clearly define your business objective. This pivotal step focuses your venture and sets the course of all future actions. Your business objective should be Specific, Measurable, Achievable, Relevant, and Time-bound (SMART). Factors to contemplate include:

1. The types of renewable energy source(s) you plan on specializing.

2. The scale of operation— small-scale local project or large-scale industrial project.

3. The targeted customer segments— residential, commercial, or utilities.

11.3. Developing a Marketing Strategy

Your marketing strategy forms the backbone of your audience outreach. Identify your potential customers, understand their needs, and tailor your value proposition accordingly. Consider:

1. Defining your target market and distinguishing your ideal customers.

2. Highlighting the unique selling points (USPs) of your offering.

3. Outlining your sales and distribution strategy.

4. Coming up with a robust digital marketing plan to boost your visibility.

11.4. Financial Projections and Funding

Develop a comprehensive financial model that captures projected income, expenditures, profit, and cash flow for the initial years of operation. Use both conservative and optimistic assumptions to exhibit different scenarios. The financial model will play a key role in attracting investors. Hence, consult finance professionals or use business plan software to ensure accuracy. Also, identify potential sources of funding: bank loans, investors, government grants, or crowdfunding.

11.5. Risk Analysis and Mitigation

Analyze potential risks linked to your venture— such as regulatory changes, technology failures, or market fluctuations— and devise strategies to mitigate these risks. Risk analysis exhibits your preparedness to handle adversities and assures potential stakeholders of your business resilience.

11.6. Building an Effective Team

Having the right people on board can make or break your venture. Define the roles and responsibilities within your team and recruit individuals who are not just skilled but also share your vision of sustainable energy. An effective team fosters a healthy work environment and catalyzes the growth of your venture.

11.7. Measuring Success

Finally, set key performance indicators (KPIs) to measure success. These could include aspects such as the amount of energy generated, number of customers served, revenue, or environmental impact.

Regular tracking and reviews can keep your venture on track, and help in quickly addressing any deviations.

Developing a business plan for your venture into the renewable energy industry isn't merely an administrative task. It's your blueprint to success, outlining your steps from the initiation of your idea to the realization of your goals. Proper planning ensures that your ship sails smoothly, even through the rough weather and turbulent seas of the business world.

www.ingramcontent.com/pod-product-compliance
Lightning Source LLC
Chambersburg PA
CBHW071032260726
48661CB00007B/3010